Chris Morgan was born in the highlands of southern Shropshire and raised in northern Worcestershire. The son of a gamekeeper, he experienced both the cruelty and joy of dealing with wildlife in the countryside from an early age.

He spent his working life as an engineer, specialising in aircraft design. This gave him a unique opportunity to travel widely and opened his mind to many foreign cultures and influences.

With a lifelong urge to write poetry, he found solace in using verse to rationalise the stress and frustration of the seemingly endless and impossible problems that we all face in this modern life. Writing it down longhand seemed to allow one at least to come to terms with many of the world's harsh realities and then to form one's own private conclusions.

Whether you agree with his observations or not, he invites you to enjoy this trip through his collection of poetry and to form your own private thoughts.

Dedicated to my son Simon who initiated my journey into publishing my poetry.

Christopher Morgan

RIPPLES:
A COLLECTION OF POEMS

AUSTIN MACAULEY
PUBLISHERS LTD.

A CIP catalogue record for this title is available from the British Library.

ISBN 978 1 78455 329 6 (Paperback)
ISBN 978 1 78455 615 0 (Hardback)

www.austinmacauley.com

First Published (2015)
Austin Macauley Publishers Ltd.
25 Canada Square
Canary Wharf
London
E14 5LB

Printed and bound in Great Britain

Acknowledgments

To my dear wife Patricia, whose patience and understanding has allowed us both to explore any opportunities for travel that came along.

To Mr Brian Luter, Mayor of St Ives, who in May 2014 bravely nominated me as the first *'Mayor's Poet of St Ives'*.

Contents

WAR

In these times of poignant anniversaries of the horrific wars of the 20th century, we gather in cemeteries attempting to empathise with our ancestors and the poor lost souls who gave their lives in defence of our realm. We are respectfully bewildered by the immense sadness that manicured cemeteries convey to us and the stark contrast between them and hideous trenches of war.

The world is a perpetual war zone; thankfully though, not yet on the scale of the last century. War is everywhere in different forms and is historically an intrinsic part of living.

It is said that getting to old age is like entering a war zone, with people around us dying off from one enemy disease or another. The difference of course is that old people have had their day and relinquish life with greater acceptance than conscripted youngsters. They 'pass away' in a gentle stream that causes just local tears, even pity for years undue.

The world wars led to the despatching of millions of our finest young men en-masse, to defend the land with a tsunami of death. The fallout of grief and pain and the ensuing depression experienced by all of the communities, on either side of the war, was immense and unimaginable for today's youngsters.

Three poems that address the devastating consequences of war.

Fields of Sorrow

I stood, in the aching voids of soldiers slaughtered,
Midst shifting shadows, of unknown heroes mortared,
At that sombre cemetery of manicured lawns.
For peace on earth they volunteered, as pawns.
Tumultuous words from haughty 'Men of War'
'Your country needs you! Come down to the fore.'
Seduced them to fight, wrenched from their peaceful helm,
To the earth's quaking line, 'Defend the realm,
You will be home for Christmas,' they did say,
Yet anxious still, our hearts await today.
Despair, the dreams, for all heroic hoards,
Dashed on fields of sorrow, by overlords
Of war, human folly, power and greed
Where a billion shells caused the world to bleed.

I drove to Dachau

I drove to Dachau to get my windscreen repaired,
Near the camp where Hitler's victims despaired.
So, with time to kill and from curiosity,
I trudged to this place of Nazi atrocity,
Startling a bird at the gate of the jail,
With a blood red throat and vein blue tail,
Singing from the tree like a nightingale.
'We don't go in there,' he seemed to say,
As he fluttered through the branches, then flew away,
From the camp.
I made for the barrack that still remained,
Out of thirty four where lives were claimed.
'This is a reconstruction,' the notice read.
There was too much left of the original shed.
Bunks were lined like cattle stalls,
Communal toilets lined the walls,
Once resounding to 'reveille' calls.
Then someone flashed a picture take,
Of a son in tears, for his father's sake,
At the camp.
With November snow piled around,
I ploughed across that fateful ground,
Past the black, twisted-steel, sculpted art,
That recalled the souls who left their heart.
The museum's bleak gallery of black and white,
Horror pictures of the fearful plight,

Haunted by Hitler's haughty sight.
People in pyjamas with a desperate stare,
Their distorted bodies and shaven hair,
In the camp.
I bought the book and left that place,
To the terrors inflicted on the human race,
Past the barbed wire moats and the concrete fence,
Where forty thousand souls lost their sense.
As I passed the gate a crow flew by,
And circled around like an alibi,
'It wasn't me,' he seemed to cry,
Echoing defences of the Dachau Court,
'I only obeyed as a soldier ought,'
In the camp.
But all that and fifty years done,
My car was fixed, the window shone,
The world around looked strangely clean,
Approaching through my new windscreen.
The camp had vanished from the scene,
And cattle grazed a meadow field,
As if the wounds had all been healed.
The midst beheld a monument,
Surrounded by a flower event.
Poppies grew along the verge,
Where people never did emerge.
And branches echoed to the lark,
Singing in the park.

Return The Stolen Years

Let me go dead on time,
When I'm due!
Not early, nor late,
But well down the queue.
For death is such sad honour,
That young heroes are born to bear,
Before the time they ought,
Leaving mothers in despair,
Bereaving in thought,
Of a spirit that once,
Was life's exuberance.
Yet others forego this noble epitaph,
For the geriatric resort,
Clinging to life's tachograph
With parchment skin and body taut,
Sunken eyes
And leaking bladder demise.
Then, when frailty meets its final relief,
We are the proud pallbearers of a corpse,
That needs no grief,
Just pity for those years undue,
That should have been more brief,
Than mercy's tardy rendezvous.
Or shared 'mongst erstwhile heroes passed
Long stolen by our warring view,
On sacrificial pyres en-massed,

When those million moments,
Their precious minds recalled,
Flooded back to steal the soul,
From where their body stalled.

FATE

The world's super-population of mankind has exploded to seven billion. It is still rising inexorably and there is probably nothing we can do about it. We are told that a country needs more people to create wealth to stay ahead of the next country. We can only speculate about the consequences of this.

Is life here on earth just a holiday? Is it a celebration of being released from the long entrapment of our own personal free atoms in the universe since the dawn of time? Finally on our passing, when our atoms are once more dispersed into the universe, can we conclude they have been on a fantastic holiday break on earth?

Poems that reflect the futility of man in the face of greater forces at work, like the weather, the consequences of the human juggernaut and day to day events we have no control over that can disrupt our lives.

The Final Pollution!

There may not be much time to go
To rid this world of overflow.
There may not be much time to spare
If all prolific nations dare,
Continue to ignore the sound,
Of overpopulated ground
And all the people that abound,
In Super Civilization.

There's never been a threat like this,
Nor ever such an emphasis.
We may not see the danger there
Beneath our own polluted air
Are we the germs upon the land
That holds us in its open hand?
Will we never countermand
Super exploitation?

There's never been less space to be
Though man usurps the forestry
Here have we so much to own
Financing with a ten year loan,
The ravage of the Earth's resource
With ever deeper probing force:
Who will live to feel remorse
For Super Charging Nations?

There's never been such great demands
Upon our planet's ravaged lands.
All around the waste piles high,
Massive chimneys paint the sky,
With fluorescent cloud effects,
Ships discharge their oily slicks
In economic disrespect
Of sea inhabitation.

There's never been such mouths to feed,
Never yet the human need.
Foliage shrinks from man's design
And species follow in decline.
Oceans bubble poison waste
And echo every whale's distaste
As we pursue in greedy haste
For Super Population.

When comes the day, as came before?
When Earth will cleanse herself once more,
Purge herself of all disease
And wash her face into the seas;
Cull the species on the land,
Or crush them in her clenched up hand,
Denuding them upon the sand,
In super retribution.

Or else the wrath of multitudes,
Divided in its human moods,
Will launch itself into the air,
Locked in flight for over there.

Cascade down around our ears,
As Earth's horizon disappears,
And freezes for a thousand years,
In super Devastation.

I came here from eternity

I came here from eternity to holiday on earth,
Thirteen billion years I waited for my birth,
Seemed like forever before I landed here,
For my holiday of sunshine as a touring sightseer,
Then it's over in a blink this brief mortality,
To passing,
From that birth, back to eternity.

Returning to oblivion up there upon a star,
Signs of my existence consigned to earth afar.
I'll be gone for evermore shedding not a tear,
Farewell my dearest progeny, I shall not reappear,
What a time I had! The school and teenage years,
Long nostalgic college days, training for careers,
Bought a big fine house, dwelt there with my love,
Children started dropping in,
And I began to see,
This holiday that I had won was first prize lottery.

Of course I must go back one day to eternity,
Where the whole wide universe is waiting there for me;
But I shall feel so blessed taking this time out,
At least I got a glimpse of what it's all about.

Egg on Your Pavement

A dozen eggs, smashed on the causeway,
Bled their stain down to the kerb.
Twelve chickens lost by tripping feet,
Smeared my path through this suburb.

I trod it to my own front door,
The yellow marks left out to dry,
A trail of yoke as never before,
Followed down the kerbs and drains,
Traffic wardens dealt out fines,
For cars that fouled those yellow lines.
And eggshells at the scene were crushed,
That shopping footfall tramped and mushed.
They stuck onto our rubber soles,
That spread them round the local street,
Wiped them on our 'welcome homes'
Those crunched-up egg shells on our feet.
Dogs would lick around the smear,
Tails a-wag and tongues in gear.
Owners snatching at the lead,
That stretched between the man and breed
But dogs are loath to pull away,
From decent smearings of the whey.

Goodbye Scotland

Fare thee well, our long-reluctant friend
Divorce is not an easy route
But best when things can't mend.
Tek the high road, we'll go low
And wave goodbye, adieu,
Raise your kilties if you like
And bare your bottoms too.
With half your nation living here
Who gets the kiddies call?
Move them back to Scotland now
And rebuild Hadrian's Wall?
Tek your oil and tek your gas, long away be gone
It wasn't us that broke the tie
Some things were always wrong.
Good luck old thing cheers to you,
Your actions may be risky
How will us Sassenachs survive
Without our tot of whiskey.
Way now join the French and that
See how well ya' fare
A thousand miles way out of it,
You'll need some extra underwear.

My Life

Was I that pigeon on the beach?
Pecking morsels caked in sand,
Flitting from the lazy reach,
Of someone's wilful throwing hand.
Only saw the underside,
Of bulging sun beds row on rows
And in between them run and hide,
Or strut around your sunburnt toes.
Footprint edits down the aisles,
Hieroglyphics typed like prose,
Between the ordered sun bed files,
By my sun-pinked pigeon toes.
And when the day had ended thus,
The pigeon flew into a tree,
Cooing at the fearful fuss,
Discharged conclusions down on me.

An Ice storm

After weeks of springtime mildness,
An ice storm passed us over,
Throwing winter fury,
Around the fields of clover.
Winds tossed blossoms to the skies,
And petal blizzards swept the street,
Smothering the concrete wastes,
With drifts of pink around our feet.
Then blackened clouds eclipsed the light,
And lightning flashed the firmament,
Thunder raged at City Hall,
That nothing built is permanent.
And ice balls fell like musket fire,
Melting first from asphalt heat,
Then gushing into milky foam,
Whilst traffic rallied to retreat.
The foam became an avalanche,
That buried kerbstones underneath,
Still traffic dared to thrash along,
Ploughing ice in disbelief.
Whoever heard the sound of ice,
Crashing into wall and roof,
Heard the wrath of Thor himself,
Testing out our weatherproof.

Then roads turned into streams of mud,
As debris slipped from higher ground,
It blocked the drains then blocked the roads,
Then choked the cellars all around.
Still sidewalks glowed with ice marbles,
Streets awash with larva flooding,
Ice balls piled at gatepost stakes,
Like frozen lumps of sago pudding.
Fire Wagons steamed, brown ice flows,
Screaming for a port to call,
Warning fools to go indoors,
'Take *shelter* from the mighty squall.'
Two hours the Heavens fired at us,
And people cowered in disquiet,
Hail fell down in Herrsching town,
In one freakish weather riot.
The sun peeped out upon the mess,
Witness to the great revolt,
Then quickly fell below the hills,
For night to quell the storm's assault.

BIRDS

Sharing this planet with the beautiful and innocent wildlife leaves us all in wonderment at our good fortune. Birds are the most free-travelling beasts of the earth, with their amazing flight and navigation skills. We are all in awe of them and worship them as the free spirits that we would like to be. Yet we feel we must interfere in their free lives wherever they are, to counteract the sometimes disastrous effect that man's modern lives have on their very existence.

Varying style poems about six birds and one mystical bird that runs our road a bit like 'Road Runner'.

There is an unexpected blockage at the end of this chapter that we are busy fixing.

Handsome Stork of the Riverbank

Reeds licked skywards on the river's fringe,
Flailing and rattling on the breath of summer,
Concealing the stealth of a ghost within,
Peeky-beaking 'twixt nervous sedges.
A massive orange bill, appeared stuck on
A white craning neck,
Unfurled from a grey body sack,
Precariously stilted above the flow.
Pterodactyl bird frozen to the riverbank,
Gawping and staring, rotating his head
And staring yet again at deep murky waters,
Deep in thought, of fish.
His proud reflection in the rippling darkness,
Single zebra strip flashed across his face,
Curving up to a dancing black fascinator,
Fluttering in the breeze over his noble head,
With a black-holed eye bored right through.
Uncombed feathers breaking in the wind,
Against the knap of his speckled waistcoat.
Then with a swift robotic strike,
His beaked arrow fires into the water
From the slender whip-lashed rope of his neck.
Twisting violently, recoiling with a breakfast fish,
Caught crossways in that excavating beak.
With a skilful toss the beak scissors open wide,
A fat silver fillet slides helplessly down,

Into the long gullet. A swollen lump,
Descends slowly down the snake of his neck,
Into the cave of his welcoming gut.
A flick of the beaked head and it's over.
Following a gentle preening of the breast.
With a knowing jerk he jumps to attention,
Proud chest swollen with the pride of his skill,
As a forlorn crow cackles in disapproval
At yet another missed meal opportunity,
Dive bombing the unmoved heron,
With a spiteful attack on this,
Unperturbed sentry of the Riverbank.
He moves away slowly, deliberating.
Cocks his great head inquisitively,
And launches airborne from a crouched jump,
Screeching a fearsome cry at the black pest,
The crow attacking, in futile dives.
With gawky awkwardness he sails away,
A dinosaur soars into the summer air,
Impressive, untouchable, majestic.

A Charm of Goldfinch

Was that a flurry of leaves
Wafting by on an autumn breeze?
Torn free from the naked beech at my garden's edge,
Like rust-etched, butterflies, flocked with scarlet,
Daring to settle upon my lawn?
'A troubling layer of leaves,' thought I,
That a careless gust would spread upon my grass
But joining their throng created such a disturbance
Of ringing, tin-belled, gold-leaf, finches,
Scalding my intrusion into their private affairs,
That they agitated to a startled, uprising flight,
Borne away on gold braided wings through turbulent air,
I had disturbed their party, so concealed myself in shame,
Behind a barrow should they deign to return;
Whereupon, a single 'goldie' alighted my fence nearby,
Beaked head twisting and turning on his mobile neck,
'King Harry's' tiny flag, waving to the throng,
With the lipstick stained face of a finger puppet.
Then, in a twinkling of cheeky inquisitiveness
He pierced me with one tiny eye,
Rotating around to pin me with the other,
To my selected spot, frozen and motionless,
I dare not move now.
He twittered 'all clear' to the flock,
Which swarmed back into my garden party,
Flitting, twig to twig and roof to lawn,

Rejoicing with nervous shifting movements,
Fleetingly delighted with my hospitality,
Then suddenly rising with a tinkling flurry,
Drawn back up to that bare tree again,
On a swirling breath of wind,
To adorn its branches as before.
The orb of that bare beech, a shoal of foliage,
Autumn glowed, from the floating finches,
Glittering, flecked-rouge and saffron-streaked feathers
Of the delightful charm of a score of goldfinch,
Adorning that lucky tree.
At least 'til wafted off, in an autumn cloud
To another beech tree of fortune,
Where golden finches briefly re-foliate,
The starkness of the trees of fall.

Kingfishers

Are bursting from the river near old St Ives,
Bringing silver treasures from their plunging dives,
Fish, trailing limply from that spearing beak,
That fires across the Ouse with a piercing squeak.

Perched on the willow twigs above the flow,
Excited by an image in the stream below,
His head starts to bob in a tango dance,
As he sights the next victim for his pincer lance.

He rears up restively and hovers by the sedge,
Fluttering in the breeze at the river's edge,
Then plops into the water like a stone from the bridge,
Emerging with a fish and water-shaken plumage.

With a squeaking cry he flies off to his nest,
A silver necklace hanging from his breast,
A flash of sapphire set in amber stone,
There's a rainbow blazed where the kingfisher's flown.

Vote Vladimir Duck

I'm a Muscovy Duck,
That's run out of luck.
The council don't want me around.
I'm ugly as sin,
Make a terrible din,
And poo all over the ground.

But us Muscovy Ducks,
Are clever old chucks.
We leave all our gluck on the ground.
Though you councillor types,
Have many old gripes,
Still littered all over this town.

So I'd like to stand,
As Mayor of this town.
No issues I'm likely to duck.
I'd have a free range,
At the Corn Exchange,
Where I'd never run-a-muck.

Three Swans Down

'There's three Swans down in the Wilhorn, Ma'am,
Felled by the hungry beast,
That hunts in the dead of night.
Heads had been ripped from their necks,
I report, they were all deceased'.

'I thought they were melted snowmen,
Three white mounds in the grass,
But all were the scenes of murdered swans,
Feathers splayed as sticky piles,
Of bones, with bare carcass.'

'Your sentries performed their duties, Ma'am,
Showed braveness beyond dispute,
Guarding the squadron even to death,
A duty they're proud to perform,
Yet more awkward, when one is a Mute.'
'We're not sure what action to take, Ma'am,
To protect the eyrar from harm;
Short of enrolling a trumpeter,
A noisy American Whistler,
Or a Whooper, to sound the alarm.'

Feathers are scattered to winds now,
Plumages blown to the skies,
Exposed are the bleached, boned remains

Where the herd continues to browse,
Oblivious of any surprise.

The Goose/Swan Serenade

There was a gawky goose,
White as driven snow,
Thought he was a swan,
As if we'd never know.
Preening with the Eyrar
Sailing with the flock,
Could hardly tell the difference,
When they came in to dock.
He wasn't well accepted,
With his orange beak,
But mute swans were afraid of him,
Because he looked a freak.
When the fleet went sailing,
He kept up at the rear,
The goose he seemed to know his place,
Ignoring all that sneer.
Two years he dwelt an outsider,
Cowering to the cob,
Squawking at his muted gang,
A rowdy goose type yob.
One day the boat show came to town,
A floodlit sail-by planned,
The polished boats in single file,
Would pass the crowds on land.
The very night the lighted boats,
Arrived upon the quay,

A gap appeared to open up,
Position number three.
The goose he gave a squawk,
The swans all mumbled so,
He flew into the gap,
With four white swans in tow.
Upstream they sailed, craft number three,
In the line of shining boats,
Two cobs, our goose, two pens astern,
In glossed white feather coats.
The papers showed the pictures,
Of the great white swan parade,
That extraordinary sail by
The goose/swan's serenade.

The Peloton Bird

The Peloton is a mystical bird
That streams down our roads. Seems absurd!
We flock to glimpse this rarest of breeds,
In the race of the latest velocipedes,
The whirring of the gears and the cowbells' chime,
Long waited hours for that magical time,
When a rare-type bird flies our roads,
With bright yellow beak and pedals for toes.
A human swarm flying in line,
Pulsating blends of colours combine.
A rainbow streaming along the street,
Above the blur of the pedalling feet.
A buzz of excitement approaches now,
Whooping, cheering, a lively row.
'There it is,' screamed a siren voice.
Now is the time to rejoice.
A distant shimmer of colours appear,
Growing like a train, approaching near.
A pulsating mass of bikes, men and hue,
Furiously pedalling, the throbbing queue.
Sweat, endeavour, human pain,
That never will pass this way again.
It streamed on by the peloton,
Flashed on through and then was gone.
The yellow jersey we glimpsed as it passed,
In sighting the peloton bird at last.

A Blockage

There's an awful lot of bilge in an old man's boat,
One sometimes wonders how it stays afloat.
When the pump is blocked by too many leaves
And the muck on his hand gets wiped on his sleeves,
As he cleans out the tube on the suction side
But the pump's intermittent, noisy as can be
A bit like the slurping when he drinks his tea.
So much like the basin where she washes her hair
Filling up the sink but the water stays there.
The plug's pulled out but I'm sorry mum,
It hangs around just smothered in scum.
Most of your hair is blocking up the drain
Wouldn't want to wear it on your head again.
Stand right back now I'll give it a pump
Got to clear out that blocked up sump
Water squirts back through the tiny overflow
Refilling the basin where it shouldn't go.
Get me some gum to block that little hole
As scum water tries to flow into our bowl.
Finally it moves and slips along the pipe
A block-relieving noise and a smell quite ripe
The water flows, one feels quite proud
All the drains are working clear and loud.
Blocked up writing is quite another thing
Don't lend me your plunger to find my zing

ST. IVES

The local government planning departments and small local shops in market towns all over Britain are battling to keep energised and focused in the face of the rapacious superstores and the effect they have on the very geography of towns. The key to retaining the soul of a town is found in recognising its rich and often forgotten history and keeping it in the mind. .

Protecting our unique and ancient culture from inappropriate progress is essential on a daily basis in every town and of course boasting about the heritage as loudly as possible.

Being *Mayor's Poet of St Ives 2014/2015* was a great privilege that was taken to heart by the author. It has led to a cross pollination of ideas throughout the town. The designation of the historic Old Riverport Area of the town has rekindled a tremendous interest, a 'sense of place' and a confidence in the town, whilst adding a romantic essence to its history.

As I was going to St Ives
I met a man with seven wives
Each wife had seven sacks
Each sack had seven cats
Each Cat had seven kits
Kits, Cats, Sacks and wives
How many were going to St Ives?

Various poems about St Ives and its surrounding area.

Holt Island (SLEPE)

There is an island in our Slepe,
That splits the Ouse's mudded deep;
And in the midst the wild abounds,
Within its willow-knotted grounds.
Warblers flirting in the reeds,
Beneath the blackcaps' fluty creeds,
Where dragonflies and damsels dance,
In the osiered ambience.
Meadowsweetened, willowherbed,
Purple loostrife, undisturbed.
Fox and muntjac languish here,
Within the thicket's ecosphere.
A duckboard winds around the isle,
That clasps this emerald jewel in style.
Strung between the winding streams,
The isle of all my wildest dreams.

Red Snapper moored on the Dolphin

If only you'd been on the Bridge
On the first day of June in St Ives,
The *Red Snapper* moored on the Dolphin
Would have set off the tongues of the wives.
It had been there the whole of the weekend
Moored tight on the quay by the Inn
But the rains had swollen the river
And a flood was about to begin.
If only you'd been to the river
And witnessed what happened that morn
Red Snapper broke free form her ropes
And crashed athwarts before dawn.
Across the arch of our bridge
She settled blocking the flood,
Sometime during the night
Her moorings had failed in the scud.
If only a witness had seen
What mystery had set loose the boat?
Smashed into our ancient old bridge
Whilst staying strangely afloat.
Aboard the *Red Snapper* a dog
Was barking away at the roof
When a face appeared at the window
And his torso at the sunroof
What's happened, I heard him exclaim
Surprise in the tone of his voice

How do we get out of this mess?
I don't see many a choice.
I turned to go to the church
Where the Mayor was being installed
And left the *Red Snapper* alone
To get himself winched from the wall.
When I returned to the scene
And the Mayor had finished his speech
The *Red Snapper* freed from the trap
Was moored upstream from its reach.
The man who'd been in the boat
Sat strumming his old guitar
Attired in his black leather coat
Singing 'swap my boat for a car'.

As I was living in St Ives

As I was living in St Ives
Awaiting bus-ways to arrive,
Each waited day rolled into weeks,
Each waited week rolled into months,
Each waited month rolled into years,
Weeks, months, years all five.
How long to get to St Ives?
25 minutes, I caught the Whippet Road Bus.
As I was going to St Ives,
I met a bus on guided drives
Each bus had just four wheels
Each wheel had just one guide,
Each guide on just one rail,
Rails, guides, wheels and drives
Whatever was going to St Ives?
Not a traction engine but a guided bus!

As I was going to St Ives
To buy myself some fish alive.
I went by boat, took over night,
I went by train, took just one hour,
I went by car and traffic jams.
By Boats, Trains or Cars arrive?
 No! Take the Bus-Way Overdrive!
Save some time, use The Guided Bus

So welcome Bus-Way to our lives
That speeds the people to St Ives.
From Trumpington, and Addenbrooke's too,
Cambridge, Histon, to ensue,
Longstanton, Swavesey, Fen Drayton Smew,
Now City, Village, Town contrives,
To take the Bus-Way to St Ives.
See Cambridgeshire with The Guided Bus!

St. Ives, Cambs

St Ives the Jolly Riverboat,
Moored upon the Ouse,
Ancient Fenland market town,
Enriched by Cromwell's views.
Founded on the livestock trade,
That drove through darkened Fens
And herded into old St. Ives,
Staining streets and pens.

The marketplace no longer brays,
With livestock's haunting tones.
The cattle went to factories
And left the buses drones,
Bringing shoppers from afar,
That bustle through and round,
Exchanging goods and livelihoods,
Within the river's sound.

Come gaze awhile this hallowed scene,
Our chapelled ancient bridge,
Two steeple-masted churches,
The Broadway down the ridge,
A Sainted, medieval Priest,
From whence the name derives,
Nine centuries of market trade
That prospers in St Ives.

The Occasional Firth of St Ives

I'm just a humble floodplain dweller,
Never been a city feller,
In the wash of mother Ouse,
The only place I freely choose,
Dilutes sloshing at my feet,
In my water-meadow suite.
The garden floods occasionally,
With water lapping at my knee.
An island nation we become
Floods all streaming round our drum
Our islet in The Ouse's stream
Raises all our self-esteem.
An Independent Hamlet free
From needy type bureaucracy.
Locals mock in futile mirth
Yet wishing so, to join our Firth.
From our dream we bear no malice,
For living with the water menace
Retains a stark reality,
That ridicules normality.
There's risk to take just living here
That keeps us in our dormant fear,
But when she floods us all around
In a post card we abound,
When Ouse becomes an inland sea
We cruise the Isle at Enderby.

Life is not how it would seem
In our isolated dream.
We raise a fist to you, defiant
For floods that make us self-reliant.
So when the next tide flushes through,
Wave us from the causeway too.
Send us down some local mirth
To St Ives' Occasional Firth,
Yet if we meet that watery end
What better way to recommend.

Brush Strokes in the Old Riverport

Faded from the pounding winter weather
And stacks of clamped, summer bicycles,
The limbs of street furniture stretched out
For their annual physiotherapy,
From the local volunteer artists.
Kneading out the knotted muscles of iron,
With deep smoothing rub-downs,
Massaging darkened skins,
With refreshing strokes of black paint.
Caressing the town crests,
With delicious strokes of gold pigment,
By the softest sweep of a hand,
Or the kiss of sunshine.
The painter's torso wrapped around,
The street furniture, in an artist's embrace,
To deliver the finest curls of colour,
To our heraldic adornments.
The road sweeper man with his broad-broom,
Swept down the causeways,
Brushing the daily dirt with a forced fever,
Flicking it onto his obedient shovel,
Whilst consigning 'bin wastes from Mars,'
To his overloaded council trolley maid,
Leant over his broom, to savour his toils,
With a 'rolled up' moment.

The mechanical road sweeper,
Followed him down with a whirring brush,
That scoured out a thousand fag ends,
From sticky kerb crevices.
A million loving brush strokes,
And the Old Riverport is restored,
To its former heraldic lustre,
With the loving adornment of this year's
Resplendent yellow floral arrangements,
Garnishing the Port's elevated floral beds,
For our coloured summer pleasures.

The Mayor Turns Around

In the month of May the Mayor turns around,
As the sun breaks through to warm the ground.
The rain can drench and the winds can rage,
In this May of hopes we replace our sage.
He swaps his robes, a ceremonial twirl
And the Mayor elect begins to unfurl.

The Mayor's turned around in the month of May,
Towards summer aspirations and fields of hay,
Facing summer solstice through the eye of spring
With optimistic hopes and desires that will bring
Brand new notions and a fresh new urge,
In the magic in the month of the May-time surge.
The Mayor turns away for renewal of his post,
With a customary whirl, to refresh our host.
For a job well done and much fulfilled,
So much accomplished, so much more to build.
A cheer ensues for the new Mayor's career,
Until he is turned around in the May of next year.

The Corn Exchange

A soul was lost in our crowded town,
The cracked shell of our revered hall,
Empty, echoing, creaking, crumbling down,
Neglected, ignored, cast aside, condemned,
By that ruthless force, distorted democracy.
Yet born again from of a wind of change,
That blew out distortions and hypocrisy,
Breathed a fresh fragrance, through the streets,
That dwells in the smiles, on the faces,
Of the thousands who enter,
The new chamber, that warmly embraces.

A String of Pearls

Hemingford Abbots met Hemingford Grey,
Along the Ouse down Huntingdon way.
Houghton witnessed from the Mill
And passed the gossip round the hill,
To old St. Ives on market day.
The babble echoed through the quay,
'Where 'twas reported,' it was said,
And next day in Fenstanton read,
Where they scripted it to verse,
So Needingworth could it rehearse
And Holywell blessed its lines,
Beneath the Ancient Ferry signs.
Earith turned it into song
And flood its banks all along.
The song swept on into the sea,
To join the mighty symphony
And now perchance it can be heard,
In the singing of a bird,
Or in the music of the sea,
That lasts until eternity.

Noses for town

As I was going to St Ives
I gave a bloke a bunch of fives.
He gave me back a bloody nose
So I fled upon my toes.
Running down the Broadway Street,
Thinking I was very fleet,
Until I crashed into a cow,
My nose looks slightly different now.
St Ives is not a violent place,
But some of us have clumsy pace.
So if our noses start to run,
Just blame it on the onion.
Ignoring everybody's calls,
I ran on through the market stalls.
It made me sneeze so violently,
Yet still my nose did not break free.
So move aside for all of those,
Who carelessly expose their nose,
Make their margin very wide,
Just in case they should collide.

Michaelmastide Reckonings

Michaelmastide,
A parochial event,
Where the harvested fields meant local content.
Broad beans and carrots with genuine crunch,
Freshly dug parsnips for Sunday's lunch,
Meat cuts from butchers fresh on the day,
From livestock nurtured in fields of hay,
Wealth was abundant in farmer's terms,
The granary full and the harvest confirmed.
The results were displayed for all to see,
Gathered and witnessed by category.

Yet the Michaelmas effect on world affairs,
Is counted in billions on stocks and shares.
It's the season for reckoning yielded wealth,
Assessing the pensions stolen by stealth.
Banks with bad debt, flogged to another,
Unknowing and trusting like old grandmother.
Have I bought a bubble or a brick built house,
A home for a king, or a hole for a mouse?
Tell me in truth don't sell me some dream
A Harvest is real and not a moonbeam.

So when Michaelmas fair rolls in for fun,
Make joy for another fair trip round the sun.
Take the Merry-Go-Round parked on the Waits

And ride the Cake-walk while it still vibrates.
Spin on the Wurlitzer parked in the road,
That's closed down to traffic for holiday mode.
Get your fortune assessed by the gypsy girl,
It's worth more in fun than a stock market whirl
And beware of the Michaelmas daisy scent,
Its fragrance is modesty, real and un-lent.

A New Bus Pass

It was the journey of a lifetime,
My bus trip to Cambridge.
Sixty years of qualification,
For the bus pass privilege.
Left my car on the drive.
An abandoned friend.
Hopped on the bone-shaking Whippet,
For my trip to the end.
'Do you take bus passes?'
'Where to?' he said
'Well, Cambridge for now,
In good time for bed.'
I was fit when we left
But how that bus shook,
Hanging on to my hair,
Not daring to look.
I stretched out a yawn,
Then to my alarm,
My teeth rattled out,
And fell on my arm.
They rolled down the aisle,
Chattering loud.
I averted my stare,
Disownment avowed.
But what am I like,
Without my false teeth?

'Are they yours?' I said.
Asking around
Goodness grief.
'You're having a laugh,'
The teenager moaned.
'They're yours, you old git
And they're probably loaned.'
'They might be' said I;
But for someone else.
So I gathered them up,
Like loose sea shells.
'Cambridge!' he shouted.
I moved from my seat,
Fell out of the bus,
Into Regency street.
Now Arbury Road's
Where I want to be,
The bright bus in front,
Was beckoning me.
Well I found myself,
In the said place,
Dentist was waiting,
A smile on his face.
Some moments later,
'That's it.' he implied
'I've finished for now.'
I couldn't speak normal,
So I mumbled a vow.
It stormed round the corner,
That Arbury bus,
And a race to the stop,

Ensued in a rush.
It stopped and the queue,
Entered the door.
'I'll catch it,' I murmured
'I've been here before.'
'You made it,' said he,
As I fell on his step,
Closed the door on my foot
With the grin that he'd kept,
'Weegen stweet prease,' I spat.
He laughed. 'Sit down there.'
Showed him my pass,
Just to play fair.
The bus to St Ives
Was a pleasure to ride
It was there in a blink
Without any guide.

Independence Day

Now me hearties
'Town not parties,'
A powerful message be,
Coined by Independent smarties
Wanting to be free,
From Tory stories, Labour's behaviours, Liberal company
Let Toby Jug join the fun
He makes more sense to me
Than all those national parties
Locked in groupery.

Again me hearties
'Town not parties,'
Shout the espirit.
Free St Ives from all those gyves
And set debating free,
From Tory stories, Labour's behaviours, Liberal company.
Our Toby Jug has more to give
Than any of those three.

What me hearties
'Town not parties?'
Birthdays, Mirthdays, Nee!!
Ban Christmas, Easter, stag nights,
Hen nights of fantasy?
Olympics stories, transient glories!

Diamond Jubilee.
Liz, Our Queen, you made us fizz, with all that pageantry.

So now me hearties
'Town not parties,'
Time to get the urge.
Build a duck board round the town
Above the muddy splurge.
Ban mud wrestling, time for testing.
Fly the flag for 'localness,'
Focalness not vocalness,
Grab the opportunity,
To make your tenure grand.
St Ives the Independent,
St Ives the Grandstand.

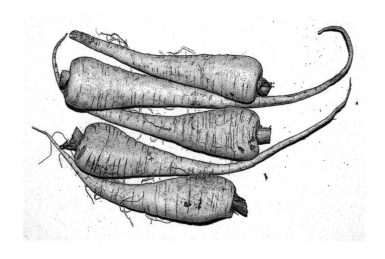

FAMILY

Just as towns are under attack from superstores, so family bonds and relationships are under attack from the incessant force of the digital and internet era. Televisions, electronic gizmos and computers have encouraged the isolation of the generations in families who shut themselves in their bedrooms, locked into a virtual world away from the rest of the family and real life.

Yet it is so important to retain cross generational relationships in order to nurture a mutual respect between them rather than to grow apart. To perpetuate and encourage these trusting relationships was imperative in ancient family cultures and should be rediscovered if lost.

Here are some poems about the effect of the family on one's whole attitude to life.

I Glimpsed My Dad in the Aura of My Son

I glimpsed my dear old dad in the aura of my son
As he paused a frozen moment, staring to the sky
Oblivious of my sighting, churning at the day
Relaxed inside a day-dream when I caught his eye.
'Hello,' said my old dad with his jaunty country tone
Ringing from his heart that quavered from the years,
He could melt a sullen mood with his golden tenor voice,
Yet, but for a Woodbine would shrink you down to tears
He heard him not my son, as he hailed to me again
But contemplated quietly, and leaned his head askew.
Dad's old voice still ringing out, his mind still in control,
Held in perfect focus by the screenplay in my view
And here we stood in limbo all three of us locked in
An impromptu type reunion where past and now impart,
Father's spirit shining through the youngster's shining face
Glowing out a warmth as he tugged upon my heart
From far beyond horizons he greeted me today
As I glimpsed upon his image, before he lost his mind,
Then he vanished in a flash as my son smiled round to me
Still unaware I saw him, before he fell behind.
'I caught a little sadness as I turned around to you.'
My son had sensed my misted eyes lost in memory,
'That's all just down to bygones, life and times that were,
Today you know I'm just so glad of your good company.'

Are you going to die Grandad?

Are you going to die Grandad?
Your hair is so grey,
With your wrinkly face
And I should say
That warts round your eye,
Are a sure sign
You may die soon one day.

Can I cook some biscuits?
In Grandma's new oven,
It's my daddy's birthday,
He's just thirty-seven.
Can I cut some cake?
For Joshie and me,
To eat as we take.

Grandma's not grey,
So grandma won't die.
She's not very wrinkly,
She said with a sigh,
Can I light the candle?
The one that plays music,
When Josh turns the handle.

Parsnips from Dad's Allotment

My old dad kept no chain on his bike.
He would wheel it uphill to his vegetable plot,
Pushing his two-wheeled walking frame.
'A bicycle mobile' squeaking for oil,
Allotment bound, up Torquay hill,
On his daily climb to his toils,
Of turning the day at his sand-soiled till
Tending his prize-winning vegetable crops
That yearned for the care of his loving soul.
He, furrowed in brow with streaming despatch
Face flushed from glares of the late spring sun
Breaking only for bread and a bottle of tea
Unfurled from a warming woollen sock.
'Ah! That juice,' he would murmur, so sure,
So warm and sweet, was all he would need.
Toiling on beyond when schools traipsed home,
On their daily migrations to and from.
Then when work was done at the dipping sun
He adorned his crossy with the freshest of fare
Potatoes and carrots piled in his basket
The sweetest of parsnips plucked from the soil
Draped on his handlebar, tied to his jacket,
Lashed with binder twine from his pocket.
With a rolling start he leapt to the saddle
And freewheeled down that mile long hill,
With the gleeful squeal of a child at play.
Scooting down valley to the street where she stood.

Legs akimbo as he rode down his horse,
With no bell aboard he shouts his approach,
'Lochinvar Riding' as folk crossed his path.
He beamed as she stood at the cottage door
'Today its fresh parsnips straight from the ground'
'I must buy you a chain for that bike,' said she.
'Why? I don't need a chain it would slow me down
When I scoots down that hill for our evenings here.'
'What will people say?' She snapped back to him.
Caring not a hoot, unloading his bike
They retired from the day for an evening within.

Goodbye Dad

I went to see my uncle,
On the passing of my dad.
Step uncle Jim from Hereford,
Where they shared their childhoods,
Along the river mad.

'You're a Morgan alright,
Yet you woon't a been 'ere now,'
He said, agasp,
'If the river 'ad took him,
Like it took young Janie
From 'is grasp.'

'E bawls to me that day,
"I coon't 'old er, Jim,
She slipped out of my 'and."
'His wrist a bleeding from her nails
That clung on to 'is band.'

'We was only playin' 'ide and seek,
But she slipped down the bank.
'E saw 'er fall as we ran off
To 'ide in nether hedge
And 'e dives after 'er a screamin,
"She's fallen off the edge."

'You woon't a been 'ere," he said,
'We 'erd 'im shout 'er name.
"Janie's fallen in!"
And we run back,
To see 'im clinging from a tree.'
'You woon't a been 'ere with me.

We pulled 'im in a bawlin.
"I coon't 'old 'er Jim.
I coon't 'old 'er 'and."
We coon't stop 'im a bawlin out.
"I coon't make the land"

'We all run down the river bank,
But she'd gone that day for good,
And 'arry, your dad, was an 'ero.
But 'e never understood.
'e sez 'e let 'er go, but 'e din't.
And YOUR lot woon't a been 'ere neither.'
Says he, his eyes a glint.

Stay In Touch

I'm not asking much,
Just stay in touch,
With your old mum and dad,
Who gave all they had,
For your upbringing.
And don't stay away
From your Grandpa's today,
He bought you that bike,
He thought you would like,
Before all the rowing.
Remember your brother,
Who lived for no other,
And your beautiful daughter,
Who once walked on water.
In the beginning.
Don't snub your friends
Make their amends,
For the wonderful time,
You spent in your prime.
Experimenting.
Don't snub your wife,
For the rest of her life,
She gave you her best,
At your behest,
Was never unwilling.

So where have you gone
My beautiful son?
You used to remember,
My day in October,
Before my late-taking.
I had to move on,
When you passed along,
So great was the pain
For me to explain,
All that upsetting.
Now I miss you this much,
But I can stay in touch,
I will join you one day,
Where you hide away,
In the unending.

My New Sister

You are our 'Lady of the Lake',
The one my father did forsake,
As he forsook had been before,
By cruel a fate as any bore,
Upon the dark side of the war.
There she stands so nobly set
These sixty years we never met.
Far away and 'over there'
Beyond the stretch of our affair,
Imagined living with despair.
The internet then brought her back
To streak across our Zodiac,
Disarming us of lifelong fear,
Her circumstance was too severe,
Yet grace herself she stands right there,
Real and normal with no care.

Domino Days

These older days they rattle by,
In my aging vintage times,
A trail of falling dominoes,
Aligned along the kerb of life,
Tumbling forth their endless rows.

Not many scraps of luck call by,
Mostly mixed-up numbers fall,
With edges worn and corners curved.
Yet when a double six is felled,
A special day in life is served,
Like grandkids visiting for tea,
Storming through our tired old house,
Ringing out their noisy rhymes,
A hope for future reappears.
They are to me the bell of times.

Their stoop is much like parents stood,
In childhood years so long gone.
A life of times ahead at stake,
Faces turned towards the door
But eyes fixed firm on Grandma's cake.
They stand so individual,
Yet underneath familiar,
The genes and traits of ancestors
Reappear in childrens' form

The family mould that reassures.

Dominoes is what I play,
Upon that old historic road,
I listen out for double six,
To fall perchance again,
To bring me back some magic tricks.

A Children's World

Oh how fast beats the heart of a child,
The intenseness of everything new.
How slow beats though, my middle aged heart,
Until I am chasing with you.
When I race you around that giant tree,
You catch me with confident ease.
Until my old heart catches up yours,
I'm not able to run in your breeze.
Time seems to speed when you pull me along,
We race through another long day
But the rate that days pass is quicker by far,
Than the ones that you stay well away.
How days drag along in my drifting times,
They all can get rolled into one,
But when you call in with such urgency,
The day speeds on past and it's done.
So please drop by as much as you can,
I care not that time will race past.
The pleasure you bring while you tear along,
Wears the smile on my face that will last.

WEATHER

Conversations in Britain have always been centred on the weather and now it has suddenly become the subject of the century on a worldwide scale. We can still be in awe of the incredible power and beauty that weather levels at us all, whilst noticing the subtle changes and warming effects and influences that our very presence has on it. Things are getting warmer as a result of our super-population but can we stop it getting worse? The two are inexorably linked but the opposing factions of peoples' beliefs worldwide work against us ever halting the process.

The Ice Melts!

There's a trillion tons of ice cubes
Hanging from our Arctic Poles
Waiting to chill the cocktail drinks
Of our lavish rigmaroles.
They hang like large umbrellas
Shielding our world from the heat
But those delicate, cracking, lamellas
Will cascade down to our feet.
Now they've started to tumble as rain,
From oceans sucked up to the sky
By the raging thirst of our sun,
To storms over twenty miles high.
There are clouds that darken the daylight
And glow like a ghostly mist
Clouds of lace-edged woven, cloth,
Draped over our Wilderness
There are clouds that smother the poles,
They cover a hemisphere through,
Clouds that reflect the fiery sun,
Attempting to hold back what's due;
And clouds with streaming, sweeping tails
Coiled back from here to New York
Delivering vengeful lashings of rain
Yet all that we do is just talk.
The spirit of life gets diluted
Once the ice melts in our drink

An ocean of rain is the consequence
That causes our shorelines to shrink.
Mankind is a massive cruiser ship
On a course fixed in destiny
Her direction can never be altered
Without yet a mass mutiny.
Ice cubes belong to the sun!
She needs them to quench her thirst
There's none to spare for greedy men
It was she started cocktailing first.
So when we have used all that ice
With our selfish and wasteful ways,
The sun will begin to reclaim
Her Earth from those profligate days.

Rainfall after Sun

There should be rainfall after sun
That scorched the bunting of the spring,
Parched the fields before they're ripe,
Threatened farmers' harvesting.
There should be Blueness after Red
Between our democratic shores,
Or vote for Orange after White,
To change the colours on our doors.
Send a storm to dampen down
The sunburnt crispness of our land,
And scent the fragrant, English air.
With perfumed rain from clouded hand.
Change the mood to sweep the minds
Of voters caught in quandary,
To ease the evil wrought before,
By some incumbent bigotry.
It should be Vernal 'fore the Sun,
To tempt some re-growth in the soil.
Where, should enterprise abound
To balance out the needy soul.

Autumnal Octobers

Autumnal Octobers
Are embedded in the fading embers
Of the long summer barbecue.
Forests, fired by the flames of fall,
Shedding blizzards of butterfly leaves
Into billowing autumn gusts.
Scorched, sun-burnt and shrivelled,
Like faces drawn around the Bonfires of Solstice,
Staring at over-cooked burger flesh.
Soon the trees are starkened skeletons
Treading deep into their annual sloughings
As they rot to their roots,
And the coals, white-dusted to the embers of the year.

The Merthyr Thunderstorm

The gentle blueness of the fading sky at evening prayer,
Blushed on the western edge from the sun's daylong glare,
Revealed nothing of the coming storm, but a wispy smear,
Of cloud and jet streams etched into the upper atmosphere.
So after the last news we retired contentedly to rest,
Falling to a sleep from which we were rudely dispossessed,
In the small hours of that morning.

A thunderstorm crashed through darkness of the night,
Awakening our slumbering world with cameos of daylight.
The crazed cameraman flashing pictures for his secret files,
Of startled landscapes and glowing rows of painted domiciles.
Frightened faces pressed against fragile window glass.
Lightning slashed at the clouded heaviness of the sky, its
cutlass
Gleaming and glinting in the savage hand of an enraged
pirate,
Chopping the sky into a hundred jagged pieces of black
velvet,
That may by chance float down and hide us from his frenzied
blade.

Then nervously counting aloud in groups of five, defying our
fate,
Thunder blasted the town from number four to number thirty-
eight.
The ramparts of the stratosphere discharged Howitzers at will,
Booming volleys of shells at the hardy folk of Merthyr Tydfil,

Cowed by the fury of the storm. The missile attack,

Cascading, meteoric explosions, from high in the zodiac,

Rocking the terraced walls of our fragile hillside homes.

The locals in terror and fear and other multiple syndromes,

Screaming helplessly at the vengeful sky.

Monsoon rains flooded down gullies in the shining, black, street,

Rocking lamps flickered and swayed attempting to retreat,

Yet caught in the silhouetted act by the flashing lights,

In the dripping, window-framed painting of the wettest of nights,

In living memory. The slumbering earth, beneath this frenzied storm,

Unmoved and reclining impassively, the dozing landform,

Hardened and unblinking, staring back at the vandals

Wreaking havoc above and the town lit by candles.

Yet little consequence to earth was such a front of violent weather,

Some lines of white washing, tangled in the drenching together,

Split tree branches bared naked to the early light of the morning,

By this fleeting pique of temper and the dawning,

That to our great earth war must have similar futility,

When all that changes in the wake of such hostility,

Are the water-coloured settings and the peoples' faces.

Autumn

September hinges summer to October,
And leaks the lingering sun through ember days.
It glows with gentler shine, the fading fire,
As rustling leaves absorb its aging rays.
Sun-burnt now and shrivelled, set to fall,
Billowing gusts will shear them from their bough,
Storms of flying leaves, take to the wind
And cascade to the lawns of autumn now.
The harvest taken early for the heat,
Leaves brush-line marks across the aching field,
Poplars mark the edges with their rows,
Pastoral England now is all revealed.
The months have moved across another notch,
Time is nigh, to wind now, back your watch.

Talking 'bout the Weather

There's very little doubt, we were having quite a drought,
Dried up and desiccated, with no water in our spout.
Quickly send some rain so people won't complain
And grasses start to grow beneath our feet again.

But give us summer sun, the good old current bun,
We all work so hard and need some lively fun.
Not too much, but warm as such,
Yet bright enough to treat us to a sunny golden touch

Farmers all a-grizzle, 'send us down some drizzle,'
They just want some weather that doesn't make crops sizzle.
Fields are just for raking, ovens are for baking,
Weather should be regulated and there is no mistaking.

Winters past were wet, summers were hot set,
Now snow storms come in June yet little rain we get.
It's all been re-arranged, the seasons have been changed,
Watching for the forecast, as if we're all deranged.

Get a nice umbrella, if you're a lucky feller,
You just cannot believe the TV rainbow teller.
Run a water butt, off your garden hut,
Collecting drops of water, when there is a glut.

Then make yourself a date, to shower with a mate,
And save a decent fortune, on your water rate.
Make social bathing plans to counter hosepipe bans,
So much fun to shower-share beneath some watering cans.

I thought that 'drying out' was alcoholic drought,
I didn't know that H_2O was what it's all about.
There's no fun drinking water, become a beer supporter,
Save the lakes for heaven-sakes, drink some brain distorter.

The Wettest Drought on Record

Have you heard the latest shout?
Forget about the drought!
It's rained the length of April
And May had best watch out.
The river's all in flood
And filling up with mud,
You wouldn't want to swim in it,
It's cluttered up with crud.

Coots are all a quiver,
Their nests float down the river.
Abandon nest or stay aboard?
It leaves them such a dither.
Forget those hose-pipe bans,
Sling out the watering cans,
Farmers will be moaning soon,
Of saturation plans.

So the Arctic's in a melt,
The ice is all a smelt,
It's taken to the clouded sky,
Then swamps our under-felt.
Forecasters of the Weather
You are so very clever.
Declared the drought to end a drought
The wettest one forever.

Take an average spring,

Whatever weathers bring.
Statistically they'll even out,
Just like everything.
Our summers are a fraud,
So we all go to Spain
And leave this special season,
To the lovers of the rain.

The Plaintive Cry of Winter

Hark! The plaintive cry of winter
In the tidings of the fall,
The Ancient Snow Queen cometh
With her soft-draped ermine shawl.
Embroidering our frosted panes
With finest silken thread,
Will she stay for Yuletide
Or yield to spring instead?
Can I be in that Christmas card?
Of frozen scenes gone by,
To skate, or fly on Santa's sleigh
In diamond-studded sky.
Don't forsake us, favoured Aunt
In your sparkling wedding gown?
Your groom is soon to join you
'Neath your frosted eiderdown.
She burnt up all our winter coal
Hung icicles from drains,
While playing in her magic dust
She stung us with chilblains.
We wore our brand new coats?
Throwing snowballs at the sun,
In this country draped in linen
Where the warming has begun.

Less often now our Aunt comes by
With winter warmness, still,
I hope she'll come to sit again
Upon my windowsill?
When last she came for Christmas
She froze the rivers here
As if to say goodbye to us;
She may never reappear.

HEALTH

Take care of your health and keep your fitness for life, but beware particularly of shingles and sneezes. They can be the most uncomfortable irritation on one's daily life.

Shingles, Jingles

Shingles, Jingles, Hell how it tingles
A terrible tiredness endured.
Pustules, hard stools,
Chuck me into cesspools
And leave me in darkness obscured.

I carry the germ of the chicken pox sperm,
Bear scars all over my head,
Spread them with sneezes
And other such diseases,
That breed in my festering bed.
So give me some pills, relieve me of ills,
My boils will no longer weep,
Send shingles to dingles,
So my life re-mingles,
And me all my sanity keep.
Just an innocent sneeze that scatters disease
To everyone stood in its wake
Is a normal reflex
A simple vortex
That causes a minor earthquake.

So ban all with shingles, jingles and ringles
Isolate all with the 'flu
Smallpox was cured
We were all assured

But shingles we can't yet undo?
It's a bit like M.E.
There's not much to see,
After that first disclosure.
A spot in the hair,
Hidden well under there,
To compromise one's own composure.
It's a bit like the measles,
Being prickled by teasels
But hides at one remote site.
So you can't skive at home,
The boss will just moan,
There's no visible sign of the mite.

Sneeze if you please

There's always a shiver that follows a sneeze
And a cough that follows a wheeze
A spot that follows a chocolate bar
And a rash that precedes disease
There's a headache that follows a late night out
And a dizziness after some beers,
A sore throat after a lengthy kiss
And a tongue lash precedes bleeding ears.
There's always a bunion follows tight shoes
A bloody nose after a fight,
A cauliflower ear from rugby I fear
And dejection after delight;
But the sneeze that escapes the hanky
Fired germs through a vortex of air
Preceding pandemics of ailments
For the whole of the world to share.
Greece just blasted a sneeze
Straight from the Acropolis
Across the borders of all the world
That started a money disease.
So watch out most carefully please
For that message from old Socrates
What floats around in the summer wind
Could lead to a terrible squeeze.

LIFE

So many varied and wonderful things happen in life that cannot be categorised. These poems fall into a generally light hearted or satirical view on many aspects of life.

A reference to Luc Besson's 'The Fifth Element' for the incredibly raw and vulnerable beauty of red headed girls. This anonymous lady dog walker became the harbinger of the hot summer of 2011.

A Rock Star came to Town to visit his mum for a weekend and put on a great guitar concert.

How great religions can abuse their followers in a manner that becomes completely acceptable for eons, until one day its evil is suddenly exposed and the whole of society heeds the hideous tales of institutionalised abuse.

Having been brought up with five sisters the author has a good insight into the strengths and vulnerabilities of women. We should all strive to keep a healthy respect for either gender. Women should be tougher with men but realise the strong effect that provocative dressing can have on a man's behaviour and the tussle he has with the force of testosterone driven impulses.

Tea Crazy

A pot of tea was stalking me,
It's not just an illusion.
She seemed to know, I need her so
And yearn her sweet infusion.
I glimpse her daily many times,
She oft, me does pursue,
That pot of tea, she fancies me
To kiss her cup of tempting brew.

I'd love a cup of tea just now,
To permeate my soul
Quench my thirst, refresh my pores,
Give me back my self-control.
I sip the cup from whence you serve
That rests upon my saucer,
The waitress smiles, she asks of me,
'Will you take some more Sir?'

My mum was expert brewing tea,
She takes my cha diploma,
Her rattling china, tinkling spoons
And pleasant tea aroma.
My milk is best poured in last,
To cause a tea-cup storm,
So when it settles, down to rest,
It's still quite hot, not warm.

I like my tea to vary some,
Different every day,
For Wednesday's cup, a steaming hot
Measure of Earl Grey.
I often like to slurp my tea,
When I am quite alone
Preferring more, to saucer slurp,
Which I do not condone.

Then I savour sleepy tea
When working day is done
Languish with you lazily
While you sip along with me
In the settling evening sun.

The 'Fifth Element'

The fifth element came for spring,
Burning up the pavements,
With her hot-looks and scorching hair,
Igniting the clouds of testosterone gas,
Hanging around our street corners,
Into greenhouse fumes, limp in the stale town air;
Then swirled by the speed of her passing,
To futile dissipation into our sky.
On she strides with the confidence
Of a fire, out-of-control in the forest
Of this early vernal drought.
Devouring Oxygen in her exuberance
In the quest for the Burning Tiger
That will smelt her conflagration
Into the sanguine contentment
Of just another suburban log burner.

There's a whole new world in a brand New Year

New Year's sparkling fireworks
Are flying in the sky,
The turning of the year has come to pass.
A wormhole opens, we jump through
The doorway into somewhere new,
A brighter world, peeps through that time crevasse.
The clocks all chime the special hour,
The countdown now is done,
Moments pause and linger in the room,
Mistakes from last year crushed beneath,
Revellers' lively dancing feet,
Reveals a space for new ideas to bloom.

We jump right off that calendar page
To let the old year die away,
And squeezing through those year-end gaps,
Enter now the Tardis Hall,
Where the world has changed for all,
Where time has managed to forestall,
And memories of the past are now elapsed.

Six Shining Guitars

Six shining guitars glowing on their stands,
Basking in the spotlights of the stage,
Waiting for the busker to come and make them sing,
Waiting for an artist to send them into rage.

Six little children waiting for the train,
Longing for to greet their mum and dad
All homeward bound from skiing holidays,
From the best of schooling trips they ever had.

On the audience waited, watching those guitars,
Slow hand-claps couldn't start the show.
Speculating, 'should we take a closer looking view?'
Of the guitars we are soon to get to know.

Instruments with twelve strings,
Instruments with two necks,
Instruments acoustic and deep bass.
Guitars of many guises, body shapes and sizes,
Standing there all lined up for a race.

Then on walks a stranger,
Looking like Lone Ranger,
Over from LA to do a gig.
'Is that his face or just a mask?
Is that his real hair?' we all ask.

'Or is it just his auntie's latest wig?'
He selects his first guitar to make it sing,
And grimaced to the pain of clashing sounds,
He strums it once again complaining of the bass,
As a sound-man joins him downstage out of bounds!
The bass came back in balance,
And the artist forced a smile,
As he strummed along some errant sounding riff,
It came right back in tune as he nodded for a while,
Relieved we were, he didn't take a miff.
The guitar finally started singing out,
The busker man had tamed it like a lamb,
He sang some blues and different hues,
That turned into a right old Rocker's Jam.
The two performing on the stage,
Guitar and legend rolling Rocker Reid,
Conjoined into a warm embrace.
Plucking out their rhythmic chords,
Heading for the rock awards
Blending there in perfect interface.

It's Too Far Out

It's far too far to go further on.
See! It's miles away round the point
And doubling back, it's just too far out,
For me with my knee out of joint.
It's too far over the sea to row
To my holiday home in the sun,
I'll go in a car a train and a plane
Though it's nowhere near such fun.

I went a bit far with you just today
Too far to know when to stop,
Our bumpers met with a fearful crash,
Now I'm worried about getting the drop.
Though going too far with your special one
Causes trauma I must admit,
The journey back to normality
Is the trip of your life, I submit.
It's never too far to deliver the truth
To anyone needing to hear.
It's sometimes too far to spit out the words,
Actions can be much more clear.
The weather here is unbearably poor,
So further from here we must go
To Spain and France, Morocco or Greece
Or to Portuguese Faro.

One in the eye

Don't look me straight in the eye
For you may, get a glimpse my soul
But you never yet earned the right to stare
Through the windows of my control.
I carry my world in my head
So don't go peeping inside
I never would look through your handbag
So don't scan my classified.

I don't peek through my net curtains,
At what should enter my world,
Preferring to be fully certain,
That nothing will take me unfurled.
It's better to read from my face,
The edited thoughts in my head,
It shows a more reasoned approach,
And masks what shouldn't be said.

I have taken to wearing dark glasses,
So I don't reveal what's within,
Though what I can still see without,
Is a world in a terrible spin.
Sometimes I stare through my bins',
To take a more magnified view,
But everyone crowds around me,
And I lose my place in the queue.

When first I looked in your eyes,
My knees just wobbled and swayed,
Your fire melted my soul away,
And my heart beats quickly delayed.
Yet now since time raced away,
I look through your windows on life,
And behold me two pools of wisdom,
That smile through the world of my wife.

Retire My Son

I have this very strong desire,
To leave my work and go retire.
For ten long years I dreamed to join that mob
You know I've done it once before
But couldn't lock that closing door
And wound up getting yet another job.
But I have been so very rash,
Spending all my petty cash
Caused me to go out and earn some more;
But this time it's the finals,
No more works urinals,
No office cakes to gatecrash like before.
They say your worth declines,
When you reach those ageless times,
And your memory is only of the war.
So while I still can just recall,
Those times we had a raving ball,
I'm stopping now so I can have some more.
So I'm going out to pasture,
Without the cash from last year,
Just eating grass and waiting there for God;
But once a while I'll take a treat
Go to town to fill my feet,
With chips and mushy peas along with cod.
And Friday nights; forgot to mention,
Just to spend my meagre pension,

I'll go and partake some cheaper beer;
But boys, I can't go buying rounds,
I would shed so many pounds,
So I'll be lurking somewhere at the rear.
So nothing's changed. I always did,
Preferring to protect my quid
And hide it well away from public view.
So to you I give some sound advice
Just to keep you looking nice,
Marry to a rich girl when you're due.

But should you ever fall in love,
With a poor lass like a dove,
Then send her out to get a job with pay.
So you will stay more young at heart,
While she plays her working part,
And you may take it easy, through the day.

Going Out

I am so glad I 'came out' tonight,
Though I gave you a terrible fright,
I was meant to be watching the football
But I just couldn't suffer that plight.
I was going to 'go out' today,
But instead I homebound did stay,
The rain was teeming, my head was screaming,
I just didn't feel at all gay.
We're 'going to' a concert to hear,
Some little known acts that appear,
Surprise was in store unexpectedly for,
An encore was called to revere.
I was 'going to do' something more careless,
Maybe I'll go out and 'wear less',
But fashion's so strict, causes conflict;
And streaking? No. I'm just far too hairless.
I guess I should 'go hide away'
For being so very risqué,
I'd have to return to my work,
To afford to be happy and fey.

It's just not your business you see,
The side that I hang's just for me,
Don't care a tot, to come out or not,
Don't really care, for I'm free.

My Two Left Feet

I am that famous footballer with two left feet.
The one that used to crash the ball,
Into the next street.
I'd always run to get it back,
'Cos everyone would 'start'
Then toss it to the other side,
From kindness of my heart.
When I was born, my mother said, I gave her such a fright.
Both my feet bent from the left,
With big toes on the right.
I learned to walk when very young,
Along with other things,
Unluckily my two left feet,
Would walk me round in rings.

My teacher used to tell me, 'Son, work behind a desk.
Keep those feet well out of sight,
They'll only make a mess.'
But I ignored his rude advice,
And slowly persevered,
Confounding experts with my skills,
Although they thought me weird.

The coaches make me practice, running down a track
But I kept on veering right and left,
A perfect dribbling knack.

'He's a proper inside left,'
The manager would say.
'Swerving all around like that
We've got to let him play.'

I couldn't be a goalie, 'cos when I jump I spin,
That makes me go all dizzy,
So I'd always let them in.
But how I bend those balls around,
Free kicks are like a dance,
Can't tell which foot will strike the ball,
The goalie has no chance.

'Do that again,' the crowds all chant,
They give me so much praise,
But I do something else instead,
That leaves them more amazed.
I can't predict how I will play,
My game's so incomplete,
I thank the magic in the toes,
Of my two left feet.

Don't Look Back

Please don't frighten the horses,
I may not relish the ride,
When the wind storms,
And the lightning strikes,
And I get this feeling inside.
I've set a respectable course,
And dare not glance to the side,
At the fullness of gowns,
And the curve of the waist,
And the bleach of the hair,
And the pout of the lips,
That has my stomach up-tied.

Don't pull hard on my chains,
As you pass with the air of a flirt,
With your long bare legs,
And extended heels,
That slink from your pelmet skirt.
I've set a respectable course
And turn away to avert,
Those flashing brown eyes,
And nonchalant smile,
The toss of the head,
And the sway of the breasts,
And your body so alert.

Don't send me right off the rails,
I can't afford to look back,
But only to swerve,
I just need the nerve,
As long as I stay on the track.
I'm trying to maintain control
But your image won't clear from my mind,
With that full summer dress,
As it falls to your knees,
And the white ankle socks,
And the dainty black shoes,
That leave me falling behind.

Don't cause me to run off the road,
I can't lose my licence today,
I just need to cruise,
I don't need a bruise,
So take your distractions away.
The dilemma will never resolve,
We only must ever submit,
To the sensuous feminine charms,
That causes our bodies to fit.
You're sonorous tone,
Just stay on the phone,
The rouge on your cheek,
That caused me to freak,
How can you do anyone harm?

Separation Online

We split on the internet today,
Conjoined for twelve long years.
Entwined by a single site address,
But confounded by complex careers.

Our hotmails were hailed with a 'Yahoo!'
In those early days of our match,
Googling away at each other,
With all of those files to attach.

The scams and the phishing online,
Friends Re-united with glee,
Us two only ever could chat face to face,
Both caught 'One-Sited' you see.

We've split up our internet lives,
From our single one-site we resign.
Now messages flow to each inbox,
And we date with each other online.
Telegraphs, telephones, iPads
And emails, mobiles and texts,
Sometimes I want to e-skype.
There's little time left for sex!
This morning she swallowed her Apple
Terribly dangerous with chips!
But she never answers her mobile!

So how can she read all my quips?

We bought a spare laptop today
So neither of us is bitter,
I mail her now from the bedroom,
And she responds with a Twitter.

We do still have mutual encounters,
But our friends all moved to Facebook.
That virtual internet city
Where messages oft get mistook.

Respect!

'I am so sorry sir. This route is "no entry."
With no nod from the owner
You may not pass the sentry.'
'Oh, you've paid up your Road Tax!
That's a plus! And insurance,
Is valid for motorways,
But your MOT's not assurance,
That your motive is genuine
And well intentioned,
As your false praises hinted,
Just now, aforementioned.'
'Wait one moment Sir!
Before you to proceed
We will check out your tyres
And if they don't succeed,
Do your indicators
Function quite as expected,
And show the true direction,
Of a route you respected?
Or whether just a whim,
Or a random direction, chosen at will
From your 'Sat-Nav' selection.'
'I am heartened to say
That your brake lights still function
But please use your handbrake,
At this special junction.'

'And now please reverse
To the "waiting" zone
Over there by the roadside,
Where drive skills are honed.'
'You may wait for ever or just for a day
But that sir is *my* choice
I'd just like to say.'

Pope of Hope

A Time Lord came to Britain
In the autumn of the year
Descending in his Pope-Mobile
A Tardis at the rear.
Anachronistic man of God
Your faith released asunder
Upon a very trusting world
That fell for all that blunder.
'Help me father will you please?
I must a sin confess.'
'Tell me quick my wretched soul
How did you thus transgress?
Come sit upon my preacher's knee
Relate to me your errors,
While I'm comforting your soul
And holding back your terrors.
Do not divulge confessions now
To anyone that asks.
It's confided just between us both
And God who set these tasks.
For if you do the Lord will strike
You from his special list,
You will be cast an "outsider"
That nobody has missed.

You knew you shouldn't interfere,
Beyond God's holy wish,
Yet that you did betraying all,
With thoughts most devilish.'
The truth is out, religious lout
So set your pigeons free,
Show us some contrition,
For abusive falsity.
Is religion just excuse,
For tainting peoples' minds?
Chaining down a person's soul,
Abusing all mankind.
For God's sake get aboard,
A secular type church,
Or poison all our children's dreams,
With medieval smirch.

TRAVEL

From a Munich tenement block to New York stardom, Madrid for a rare curry house and a windsurfing holiday in Sete France, all inset with an obscure view of the traveller in general.

Tenemented Times

This gorgeous, pouting, crimson rose,
You planted in my fourth floor balcony dirt,
To shed tears at the morning sun,
Down its blood red cheeks,
Petals occasionally fainting to the ground,
On a flirtatious waft of summer wind,
Whispering tales of untold beauty.

The rose we nurtured through those glorious years,
Draped now along our elevated balcony,
Like last night's ball gown,
Airing away the smoke of the evenings of fun
And colouring the austerity of
Our stark grey monument,
That soars above the autumn mists.

And their blazing hues flash across green canyons,
Yawning between our monolithic dwellings,
Triumphant arrays of petunia shine back,
Signalling the coloured camouflage of normality,
Passive acceptance of packaged families,
That sometimes wave to shore,
Like transient souls departing port on that last ferry.
Elevated floral displays,
Gardens hanging from the thirteen decks,
Of our cul-de-sac into the clouds,

Defying normal laws of nature,
With people-stacking, sky-scraping blocks,
That sometime will crumble like the gravestones,
Gathered around our ancient Saxon churches.

Beauty is that fleeting apparition,
Of unusual and natural energies,
That focus into glorious displays,
But more seldom do they reappear,
As our heads sink deeper into the dirt,
That will eventually swallow everything,
And leave a futile seam of archaeological evidence.

So we celebrate every ephemeral image,
Of beauty we are privileged to behold,
In this grey-towered conurbation,
That shelves our condominiums,
Somewhere in one of those brick drawers,
That stack up to the sky,
Like human warehouses.

New York

America's eastern mountain range!
The aspirational peaks of New York,
Dwarfing the suburban pizza of Long Island,
Piercing the clouds of mass imagination.
Sun glinting on the glazed snow caps,
Of the Matterhorns of Manhattan.
Emperors of the State,
Striding boldly into the sky of men's minds.
Majestic towers, chiselled skywards
From sacrificial neighbourhood rock.
Aloft, midst this noble gathering of giants,
Vertical extrusions of granite,
Designed for spacious capacity,
In this sprawling pancake city.
The East Coast Event Horizon,
To tumble into and return a star.

The Traveler

The traveler is the strangest beast,
Moving adroitly from west to the east.
Clamoring for that extra ingredient,
To justify something extra, they needn't!
Until they are contrarily sure,
That there is no other hidden door,
Left to reveal a mind that could be broader,
Or more circumspect than the general order.
They need to amaze all humanity,
With their expeditions of insanity,
Photos of rocks, photos of towers,
Photos of strangers, photos of flowers,
When the world has only respect,
For carbon footprints of an insect.
Soon there will only be
Photos of misbehaving weather,
With all of us huddled together,
In some corner of our earth,
Where we hunker down in our dearth,
Of the normal expectations,
From violent religious disputations,
Where thoughts and godly ideas,
Are wrecked on the rocks of intolerance,
By bigoted canons of in-sufferance
And the bullying dogma of mankind.
That was all the traveler could find.

A naan bread for breakfast

It lay in the fridge alone and obscene.
I had fallen off the late shift, through a week
Gorged on tortilla, cardboard bread and instant cuisine.
My pallet yearned for some Eastern Spice,
So I headed to the evening curry sales,
Spurred on by a vision of masala and rice,
Inspired from savouring two strong ales.
'The Taj' was pristine with Eastern guile,
The deferential waiter sat me alone.
He brought me the menu; 'In Spanish,' he smiled
And left me to struggle while he answered the phone.
The listing was standard familiar and long,
Dhansak, Tandoori, Balti and Korma
And my favourite of all the lamb Rogan,
In a sauce laced with cream. That's so abnormal.
I'll start with Masala, chicken Tikka
And a Kingfisher beer to quench my thirst,
A poppadum with sauces and pickle,
Peppered and crispy. My lips pursed.
Deliciously followed by Chicken Masala
And the Pilau rice with the Rogan Josh,
A thought crossed my mind. 'I could hide in the parlour,
And OD on curry,' though I'd have to be hushed.
'A table for eight,' boomed a Brummie voice.
The deferential waiter led them just so.
An Indian family here out of choice,

Discussing the menu, as only they know.
'We'll have four number threes and two twenty twos
And eight number sixes and four forty fives.'
'They think they're all at the bingo,' I mused.
In an Indian restaurant in Madrid in their lives,
They'll visit but once, I'll hazard a guess,
Then not to order in their native tongue!
The deferential waiter attempts to assess,
With a puzzled look, it all seems so wrong.
I stared at my glass and ventured to think,
'This must be good beer.' I was laughing inside,
Finished my drink,
Paid up my bill and ordered my ride.
Whilst leaving this cultural melting pot,
The Indian family all glanced at me,
I bade them goodnight with my breath awfully hot
'Adios,' said I, 'You should try thirty three.'
So how this naan had entered my fridge,
I haven't a clue but breakfast is free,
It must have followed me over the bridge,
In the doggy bag by my cup of tea.

Caught between things!

Down where the wind slips over the sea,
And dorsals cut the deep.
Between the restless mantle of air,
And the swell of Neptune's Neap.
On darkened lace that rain splash weaves,
Across the mighty Ocean plane,
Where puissant bombs can trampoline,
And mighty ships contain.
There is a strata,
Of precipitated power,
A seam of Einstein's energy,
Floating like a flower.
A jet-stream force that sailboards ride
And hovercrafts deploy,
That thrusts them into hyper-speeds,
Across horizons warping line,
To new dimensions, solitude.
Down between the air and brine,
Where two great elements combine,
Upon the ocean's very shine,
The surface of the sea.